EVERYBODY EVANGELIZES

ABOUT SOMETHING

EVERYBODY EVANGELIZES
ABOUT SOMETHING

MATTHEW KELLY

BLUE SPARROW BOOKS
North Palm Beach, Florida

BLUE
sparrow

ISBN: 978-1-63582-159-8 (hardcover)

Designed by Ashley Dias
Cover Photo by Brian Kinney

10   9   8   7   6   5   4   3   2   1

FIRST EDITION

Printed in the United States of America

TABLE OF CONTENTS

"The harvest is great but the laborers are few."

Matthew 9:37

PART ONE

EVERYBODY EVANGELIZES about something. Some people evangelize about their favorite restaurant or vacation destination, others about music or a movie, some about their new iPhone, and still others, about a politician or political agenda. Everybody evangelizes about something, and everyone is a disciple of something or someone.

There are now 2.5 billion iPhones on the planet. That didn't happen without some serious evangelization. And there have been many times when I have heard people speak with great passion about their new iPhone and thought to myself, "Imagine if Catholics were this passionate about sharing the Gospel!"

It is in our nature to evangelize. It is in our nature to share good news with others. Those who have had a deeply personal encounter with Jesus do not need to be told to evangelize: it is an inevitable consequence of that encounter. If you place an empty bucket under a dripping tap it will eventually overflow. It has no choice.

Though we have traveled different paths, we are each here today because we have accepted God's invitation to serve his people.

I was raised in Sydney, Australia. Each Sunday I went to Mass, I attended Catholic schools, and I received the Sacraments. And yet, although I had been immersed in the activities of our faith, like millions of my generation, my heart had not been won for Jesus and his Church.

I knew about Jesus, but I did not know Jesus–and knowing about someone is not the same as knowing that person. This is the difference between catechesis and evangelization.

When I was fifteen I was evangelized. My path crossed with a man who challenged me to pray and read the Gospels, reflect on the larger questions of life, and consider my responsibility to the poor and lonely. He patiently answered my questions about life and the faith. It was at this time that I encountered Jesus in a deeply personal way. The direction of my life was forever altered.

As I delved into the Catholic experience, one idea captured my imagination above all others. It was the idea that holiness is possible and that each moment is an invitation and an opportunity to grow in holiness. It was the first time holiness had been set before me as a possibility. Each moment was now filled with purpose and each moment grasped for God produced an explosion of joy in my soul.

When I began speaking and writing about the faith in my late teens, I wanted to share this joy with others. By that time, I had immersed myself in the documents of the Second Vatican Council and was convinced that the universal call to holiness held the key to helping people find meaning and purpose in their lives, and the key to helping them understand the genius of Catholicism.

Over the next seven years, I visited the Church in more than fifty countries speaking to people of all ages. Standing before audiences I noticed that when I began speaking about the universal call to holiness their eyes would glaze over. There was a disconnect. This was magnified when I visited high schools. Standing in front of a thousand teens you can tell how each and every sentence is received, and the concept of holiness was simply unable to capture their attention.

I didn't know it at the time, but now I realize that the reason they were unable to engage in a conversation about holiness was because they had already fallen victim to the biggest lie in the history of Christianity. It is not a lie that non-Christians tell about Christians, but rather a lie we tell ourselves: "Holiness is not possible for me." This is the lie that hundreds of millions of Catholics have accepted consciously or unconsciously. This is the lie that has paralyzed the inner and outer lives of Christians in the modern world.

When I first started speaking and writing I found this incredibly discouraging, because I wanted others to experience the joy that I was experiencing by immersing myself in relationship with God and this quest for holiness. So, I began to experiment with language.

How could say it in a way so they could hear? How could I set them free from all the false stereotypes and caricatures about holiness? How could I explain it in a way that cut through bias and prejudice? How could I help them to hear the message as a beautiful invitation to a new way of life?

It was out of this search that the phrase "the-best-version-of-yourself" emerged. I can still remember the first time I used it. At the time I was traveling and speaking more than two-hundred days a year, and one night, speaking to a large group at a church in California, it came to me.

"God has an incredible dream for you," I said, "He wants you to become the-best-version-of-your-self!" Their reaction was instantaneous. I could see in their eyes that they had heard the message in a new way, that it had captured their imaginations. I went on to explain that some things we do help us to become the-best-version-of-ourselves and others do not. They understood clearly. It was as if I could see their minds filling with examples they had identified for themselves. I explained that some things we do help other people become the-best-version-of-themselves and other things we do prevent people from becoming all God created them to be.

For the past twenty years, I have lived in the United States and dedicated myself to serving the Church there. Since first arriving in the United States, I have visited more than three thousand parish communities. These visits convinced me of our desperate need for powerful catechetical and evangelization programs that inspire the people of our times to embrace the life-giving ways of the Gospel. For the past decade I have focused on developing catechetical programs with the incredibly dedicated team at Dynamic Catholic.

In each of these contexts, the concept of becoming the-best-version-of-yourself has played a critical role in engaging the people of our time in a vibrant conversation about entering into deep relationship with Jesus and his Church. But the concept is the result of striving to find language that attracts, resonates, invites, encourages, and challenges people in a way that they can hear.

In every place and time God desires to awaken new forms of Catholic creativity. Some eras embrace it, some ages reject it, some ages persecute it. The question is, are we open to a new era of Catholic creativity and imagination?

Language may be one area where God is calling us to unleash this creativity, so that we can reach the people of our age, especially those who seem most unreachable. Both witness and language play pivotal roles in the process of evangelization. Witness speaks the language of all men and women in all places and times. Language is burdened with greater limitations.

It is the limitations of language that require us to continually revisit its effectiveness.

Language engages or disengages. It encourages or discourages, creates clarity or confusion, unites or divides, is constructive or destructive. It invites people or alienates them. Language can be casual or formal, humble or arrogant, effective or ineffective.

In one way or another every topic we have discussed this week deals with the effectiveness of our efforts to carry out Jesus' mandate to his disciples–his mandate to us (Mark 16:15). In our efforts to share the Gospel with all men, women, and children to the ends of the earth it seems the Holy Father is inviting us to examine and question our effectiveness. It is a bold challenge. Will we meet it with fear or hope?

Reflecting on the effectiveness of our efforts to evangelize will require all the courage we can muster.

During the early days of the civil rights movement, which sought equality for all people regardless of the color of their skin, James Weldon Johnson wrote, "We need to hold a mirror up to this country." Ever since Pope Francis stepped onto the balcony here at Saint Peter's Basilica on March 13, 2013, in almost everything he has said and done, he seems to have been saying to us: We need to hold a mirror up to ourselves. We need to hold a mirror up to the Church. This can be frightening, because mirrors don't lie.

It is a bold challenge. One that we can all avoid with the busyness of our lives, even the busyness of ministry. Even this week, here in the context of this gathering at the Vatican, where if nothing else we should courageously explore and boldly discuss the effectiveness of our efforts, it would be ever so easy to speak about everything but this critical issue.

How effective has the New Evangelization been to date? Do we have the faith and the courage to face this question with rigorous honesty?

On the most basic level we discover our failure by randomly asking a dozen Catholics, even those who attend Mass faithfully, "What is the New Evangelization?" This will almost certainly be met with a dozen different answers, or worse yet, blank stares and shrugging shoulders.

The average Catholic doesn't know what the New Evangelization is, and the average Catholic doesn't know how to participate in it.

Since Pope Paul VI first proposed the New Evangelization in his 1975 apostolic exhortation, *Evangelii Nuntiandi* his dream has been expanded on and promoted by John Paul I, John Paul II, Benedict XVI, and now Francis. For twenty-five years, during the papacies of John Paul II and Benedict XVI, there was no more dominant theme. And yet, in holding a mirror up to our efforts to evangelize the modern world, how successful do we believe we have been? An honest exploration of this question leaves us humbled by what we discover.

There are of course reasons for our failure to engage the people of our age, but do those reasons lead us to the self-satisfied righteousness of justification, or do they jolt us to search for new and more creative ways to evangelize?

Our failure is twofold. Our efforts to evangelize the modern world have failed in witness and language.

In *Evangelii Gaudium* our Holy Father wrote, "the Catholic Church is considered a credible institution by public opinion, and trusted for her solidarity and concern for those in greatest need" (65). In the six short years since this document was written this has tragically become less and less true. Countless Catholics and non-Catholics no longer see the Catholic Church as a credible institution worthy of their trust. This produces a significant obstacle to all our efforts to evangelize as trust and respect are essential to the process.

The faith has always been most effectively spread through the trust, joy, and respect of friendship. If you want someone to hear a truth they don't want to hear, the most effective person to deliver that message with success is a friend for whom the other person has mountains of trust and respect. Too many people no longer see the Church as that trusted and respected friend.

This makes it all too easy for people to fall into the trap of believing that the Church is irrelevant and breeds the greatest enemy to evangelization: indifference.

We can deny this, argue about it, parse it by degree, ignore it, or look deep into the mirror and realize our failures. Our failures will then teach us to go forth more determined than ever to win back that trust and respect, so that we can effectively invite more people than ever before into a life-giving relationship with God and his Church.

This will require authentic witness and a new language.

We live in an age when much of our language pushes people away rather than drawing them nearer to the living God. The very language that should unite people with their Creator has become an obstacle awkwardly wedged between God and his people. This is unfortunate, and no doubt uncomfortable to admit, but it is so. The question is, how will we respond? Will we stubbornly cling to language that simply does not work and complain about the fact that people have become so disenfranchised from God, religion, and spirituality by modern secularism? Are we satisfied having the right words in the right place even if millions are unable to hear those words in a life-giving way? Or will we open ourselves to new language that enables us to fulfill our mission more effectively in this place and time?

Many people are allergic to Church language. If someone is allergic to a medication, you don't give them that medication. But you also don't refuse them medication altogether.

If we continue to see language as an end in itself, rather than as a tool with the specific purpose of leading people closer to God, our efforts to evangelize are unlikely to be any more successful. But language is a tool. It exists to communicate, to engage people, to educate people, and to inspire people. Language serves God by serving his people.

At this point, let me say that I am open to being wrong. What matters most is that we begin this conversation and others like it. I may be wrong.

We may find a new way to accomplish our mission with the old language. What we need to do is stop avoiding the conversation. When we refuse to engage in conversation we close ourselves off from the world.

Surely our faith is not so fragile and weak that it cannot stand up to vigorous conversation. Even when it comes to "settled questions," we should not be afraid to engage in conversation. We should in fact welcome conversation as an opportunity to help people more fully understand the genius of our Catholic faith. For a question may be settled theologically or dogmatically, but if it is not settled in people's hearts they need and deserve as much conversation as necessary to work through that question.

Evangelization is after all a conversation between the Church and the world, between each baptized Christian and the people in his or her circle of influence.

Today, the phrase "the-best-version-of-your-self" has become ingrained in popular culture. Football coaches use it at press conferences, movie stars use it in interviews, business leaders speak about helping their people and their organizations become the-best-version-of-themselves, and millions of parents ask their children every day, "Will what you are about to do help you become the-best-version-of-yourself?"

For whatever reason this concept and language resonates with people of all ages, and provides insight into what is possible.

There is light and hope when we realize that this problem we face is not entirely new. The Church has been translating the Gospel into new languages for two thousand years.

Saint Jerome translated the Scriptures into Latin to make the message accessible to as many people as possible, but he also wrote commentaries to provide even more accessibility and clarity. How effective would our efforts be today if the Church only communicated in Hebrew and Aramaic or Latin?

Over the centuries, hundreds of scholars have worked tirelessly and often anonymously to translate the Word of God into every language under the sun. The challenge before us today is to translate God's message into a cultural language, which is infinitely more difficult than translating it into French, Swahili, Chinese, Arabic, or English.

Dynamic Catholic is a grass roots lay ministry committed to re-energizing the Catholic Church in the United States. While it is a young organization, just ten years old, it has been incredibly successful at engaging disengaged Catholics. There are fifteen thousand parishes in the United States today. Last year, more than twelve thousand of those parishes used at least one of Dynamic Catholic's catechetical or evangelization programs. During Lent and Advent almost a million people will visit

DynamicCatholic.com each day to view our daily video reflections. I am often asked what the secret to this success is, especially in light of the fact that it seems to be harder and harder to reach Catholics in the current culture.

From the beginning we have used a phrase, *"Meeting people where they are and leading them to where God is calling them to be!"* Some people see it as just a marketing tagline, but it is much more than that. This concept is at the heart of effective evangelization. And while it is an idea that many have adopted from us, while it is easy to speak about, it is incredibly difficult to accomplish in ministry.

One of the mistakes that has plagued our efforts to evangelize and catechize the modern world is our tendency to misread where people are in the adventure of life, where they are in their spiritual journey, where they are in their ability to understand the life and language of the Church.

We assume people know more than they do.

We assume people are more committed than they are. We assume people understand the language we are speaking, yet often they have no idea what we are talking about. These false assumptions are massively undermining our efforts to lead people into deeper relationship with God. As a result, we are often answering questions people are not even asking, and ignoring the questions their hearts and minds are preoccupied with.

Perhaps the most dangerous assumption we are making is that the people in the pews have been evangelized. Over the past decade, Dynamic Catholic has developed catechetical programs for each of the sacraments. In the process we stumbled upon a significant discovery. Throughout the catechetical journey that a Catholic experiences if he or she was baptized as a child, we assume that he or she has made a choice and commitment to Jesus and his Church. This simply isn't true. The sacramental reality and the practical reality are not aligned. This is not an intellectual or theological assertion, but rather, a nonjudgmental observation. Although people have experienced most of the sacraments, the fruit of their lives tells a different story. Their lives do not announce to the world, "I have made a choice and commitment to walk with Jesus and his Church." And yet, the great majority of catechetical materials are developed based upon the false assumption that participants have made this commitment.

You cannot catechize the unevangelized. They need to be evangelized before they can be effectively catechized. For this reason, many of Dynamic Catholic's programs have a very different starting point, because the capacity and desire of the unevangelized to absorb catechesis is very minimal.

This effort to meet people where they are and lead them to where God is calling them to be has also led to another discovery, which is both astounding, and yet, upon reflection unsurprising.

More and more people in society are in need of a pre-evangelization experience before they can be evangelized and catechized.

My parents taught me to work hard, be honest, be happy for other people when they succeed, and to care for the poor. My brothers and I grew up in our parents' love and care. This provided a natural foundation of goodness. The Gospel takes root very easily in that foundation of goodness, but fewer and fewer people are being given this foundation of goodness by their parents. Rather than being raised on hope and joy, they are raised on selfishness and enter the world afraid and questioning. These people need to be loved into a place of hope, so that the natural virtues of goodness can be nurtured in their hearts and souls. This is the pre-evangelization I speak of. Only then can the rich seeds of the Gospel take root in their lives.

Returning for a moment to our misguided assumption that people have made a choice for

Jesus and his Church. There is another way this assumption undermines all our efforts to evangelize, and it is immensely practical. The unevangelized cannot evangelize. It isn't because they are lazy, or ignorant, or bad people. It's because it simply isn't possible. You cannot passionately introduce others to a life-changing person and message if you have never experienced them for yourself. So, when we ask the unevangelized to join the New Evangelization it is an exercise in futility. This is why they look back at us with blank stares.

The most basic educational methods inform us that connecting new information to existing knowledge is essential to success. If a child enters a third-grade math lesson with a first-grade working knowledge of math, he or she is unlikely to learn very much at all. It is therefore critical to know where a student's current knowledge stands so we meet them where they are.

In order to meet people where they are in the

process of evangelization, we need to know what occupies their hearts and minds. The reality is most people are worried about something and hurting in some way.

What's on people's hearts and mind? Money problems: They are struggling to pay the bills, drowning in debt, have a job they hate or no job at all. Health issues: They are sick or someone they love is sick. Marriage problems: Their marriage isn't working, their spouse doesn't love them anymore, or they have a good marriage but don't know how to make it better. Children: They have a child they are worried about, or they desperately want to have children but cannot conceive, or they want to be better parents but don't know how. Addiction: They are addicted to something and are desperately afraid someone is going to find out, or someone they love is struggling with addiction. Self: They don't know who they are or what they are here for, they feel lost and afraid, their life lacks meaning and purpose, but they are afraid to share that with anyone. And these are high-class problems compared to other problems that our Holy Father addresses in *The Joy of the Gospel.*

And yet, whatever their joy and whatever their burdens, they share one thing in common: the unchanging human need for healing and wholeness. This quintessential human yearning does not change, but people no longer look to God and his Church to deliver the healing and wholeness that they thirst for unquenchably amid today's secular culture. They know their lives are not working. They know that something significant is missing. They are living what Thoreau described as "lives of quiet desperation," but they don't understand that God, religion, and a vibrant spiritualty are essential to their happiness.

And so, the challenge for the modern disciple is to go to the people, to meet them where they are, both literally and metaphorically. This is where the indispensable role of the laity in the New Evangelization is highlighted. The laity are constantly moving along the highways and byways, passing through the marketplace and every professional environment, and enjoying places of recreation and entertainment. It is here that the great moments of opportunity to evangelize exist.

It is the casual encounters between the evangelized and the unevangelized that are rich with possibility. They are not opportunities to preach, but opportunities to live and love, to listen and bear witness to the joy God has filled us with *the joy of the Gospel.*

This approach has its roots in the ministry of Jesus. As we reflect on his life and ministry it is no small matter that he almost never preached to someone before he had met a very human need. He first fed, healed, encouraged, and comforted people.

Theodore Roosevelt, the twenty-sixth President of the United States, famously said, "People don't care how much you know until they know how much you care." The people of today want to know how much Catholics and their Church care. They are sending us a very clear message, "Don't tell me, show me." They are tired of the lectures and preaching. They yearn to see someone, anyone, actually live the Gospel in the midst of this modern secular culture. Somewhere deep inside, we all want to know it is possible.

Love of neighbor is always triumphant. While secularism poses many challenges to our efforts to evangelize, it has become so pervasive now that people are surprised by genuine Christian love, compassion, and generosity. We have an opportunity to juxtapose the Christian life authentically lived with the emptiness and selfishness of secularism. The first Christians used the same juxtaposition to intrigue the people of their time. When the Gospel is lived, it still holds the spellbinding power to capture the imaginations of the people of any place and time.

Our enemies can attack the Church in a thousand ways, but there are some aspects of our faith that are untouchable. My favorite is this: There is simply nothing more attractive than holiness. When somebody actually lives the Gospel it is incredibly attractive, and not just to Christians. Who loves Francis of Assisi? Just Catholics? No. Just Christians? No. Men, women, and children of all faiths and no faith. Why? Because there is nothing more attractive than holiness.

What is the source of this holiness? The Lord himself, of course. But in practical terms it all comes down to living in the presence of God. This is the source of our life, love, and joy. David danced for joy before the ark of the covenant, he danced for joy in the presence of God. John the Baptist danced for joy in the womb of Elizabeth acknowledging the presence of God when he heard Mary's greeting. A life lived in the presence of God is a joy-filled life. But so many things can drag us away from God.

Those of us who have dedicated our lives to ministry need to guard our joy in a special way. Too many people in ministry have lost their joy. And perhaps the ugliest thing in the world is someone who is serving others and trying to bring people closer to God, but has lost his or her joy.

The challenge is ever before us to animate the Gospel for the people of our age, so that we can effectively invite people to make the transition from tourists to pilgrims, and from consumers to disciples.

There is so much more that could be said, but my time has elapsed. So, I will leave you with this thought: The Church is not something we inherit from generations past or take over from our predecessors. The Church is on loan to us from future generations. The Church exists for people, people don't exist for the Church; and we have a responsibility to the children of God, not only here and now, but to every generation until the end of the world.

This may seem daunting and at times the obstacles may seem insurmountable, but let us never forget that the ways of truth, goodness, generosity, and love always triumph when they are lived. If this is the language of our lives, it will be impossible for us not to attract people to God.

Matthew Kelly
The Apostolic Palace
Vatican City
November 30, 2019

PART TWO

IMAGINE FOR A MOMENT that by some mysterious power you were able to change the world. What would you change? How would you change it? Superheroes use their power to outwit the bad guys. When songwriters assign themselves the power to change the world, they often use it to win the love of the one they desire. Getting rid of the bad guys is certainly fine and noble, as is love, but surely if we could change the world, we should use that power for the greatest impact.

How would you change the world? Perhaps you would eradicate poverty, disease, and ignorance, or put an end to war, famine, and all the useless violence and destruction that we inflict upon each other.

But changing the world is an inside-out job. When we look to change the world, too often we look outside ourselves. When God looks to change the world, he looks deep within us, driving straight to the heart of the matter: human behavior. The world is the way it is today because of human behavior. The world is changing, constantly, for better or for worse. The way we live our lives today makes it better or worse tomorrow. There are seven billion people on the planet. If your life were multiplied by seven billion, what would the world be like?

The world only changes for the better when men and women grow in virtue and character. Less virtue can never lead to a better world. Less character will never lead to a better world. Our lives genuinely improve only when we become better people today than we were yesterday; the destiny of the world is wrapped up in this deeply personal quest.

In the book of Exodus, we read the story of Moses leading the people out of slavery and into the promised land. God wants to do the same for each and every one of us. He wants to lead us out of our slavery, whatever that is for you and me, and lead us to the promised land of a life filled with passion and purpose. But along the way, despite the incredible things the Lord had done for the Israelites, they turned away from God, became discontented and filled with entitlement, and began to argue among themselves and divide as a community.

What did God do? He offered them a fresh start, just as he offers each of us a fresh start today. But that fresh start was not based on ideas or philosophies. It was based on a new way of living. God invited them to change the way they behaved. He essentially said, live by these Ten Commandments I place before you today and you will live rich, full lives in friendship with me . . . and the world will be a better place for everyone. It is amazing how timeless those commandments are.

1. You shall love the Lord your God and serve him only.

2. You shall not take the name of the Lord your God in vain.

3. Keep holy the Sabbath.

4. Honor your father and your mother.

5. You shall not kill.

6. You shall not commit adultery.

7. You shall not steal.

8. You shall not bear false witness.

9. You shall not covet your neighbor's wife.

10. You shall not covet your neighbor's goods.

I know it may seem a little old-fashioned, but wisdom is always old-fashioned. Let me suggest a small exercise. Watch the news tomorrow night with this list in front of you. As each story is presented, usually misery after misery, consider which of these ten have been broken. In the great majority of cases, wherever you find injustice and misery in this world you find that at least one of the Ten Commandments has been broken.

Imagine all of the misery that could be avoided if we all just lived by these ten nuggets of life-giving wisdom. Think for a moment on all the suffering that is caused because humanity has been unwilling to adopt a pattern of behavior and a social structure that celebrates the wisdom of the Ten.

The world needs changing, today as much as ever before. Most people agree the world is a bit of a mess. I don't know anyone who would say it is in great shape, on the right track, changing unequivocally for the better. Parents seem universally concerned about the world their children will grow up in. When I speak with grandparents, they often tell me that they don't like to think about the world their grandchildren will inherit because it makes them too anxious.

Sure, we have explored space and invented the Internet, but one-third of the world's population is starving and the moral-ethical foundation of our society is being demolished before our very eyes. We have more and more of what we want, but less and less of what we need.

The world is a bit of a mess, but we abdicate the responsibility for this in two ways: We convince ourselves that the state of the world is someone else's fault, and we convince ourselves that it's someone else's responsibility to fix. We are wrong on both counts. Even sadder is the fact that more and more people believe that the world cannot get better. The truth is we are all changing the world. Every word, thought, and action changes the world in ways that echo throughout history, touching people and places you will never meet, for ages to come.

Most people agree the world is a bit of a mess, but as Christians we refuse to believe that it must be so. We believe something can and should be done about it, and that we are called to play an active role in the transformation that is so obviously needed. We are called to be especially mindful of the role we play in changing the world.

This is particularly true for Catholics. Our mission as Catholics is not merely to move through the world, leaving it unchanged. Changing the world is part of our mission, and throughout history we have done that in many ways. The Catholic Church broke the class barrier for education. We invented the scientific method to transform the sciences. We have always been a leader in caring for the sick and the poor. In almost every place and time for the past two thousand years, the Catholic Church has played a powerful role in making the world a better place. Catholics change the world.

It is, however, important to remember with heavy hearts that our influence has not always been positive. Catholics have affected the world in horrible ways also: the persecution of Galileo, the burning at the stake of Joan of Arc and others, the atrocities of the Inquisition, the persecution of so many saints, and the sexual abuse scandal within the priesthood. But even in the face of these horrific contributions to history, it is impossible to argue that the Catholic Church has not been a force for good around the world for two thousand years. It is also important to note that when we have failed it has always been because we did not live our Catholic faith authentically.

Imagine for a moment if the Catholic Church had never existed. Could you even count the number of people throughout history who would have starved to death, the number of people who would never have been educated? How could you measure the influence of all those the Church has raised up? How do you measure every kind word of encouragement and good deed that has been inspired by the Catholic faith? Can you even imagine removing all these from human history? And if we could, what kind of a world would we find ourselves in today?

There are a growing number of people who think the world would be a better place if the Catholic Church had never existed. I pray you and I can live lives that discredit this argument more and more with every passing day.

Changing the world, now that is something worth getting excited about. But how often do you walk into church and think to yourself, "This is a group of people focused on changing the world"? I have been around groups of people who were trying to change the world and I have been around those who were simply trying to change their business or industry, and I can tell you that the energy that those groups of people exert is very different from the energy we exude as Catholics at the moment. It may be an oversimplification, but the reason for so many of our problems and inefficiencies at this moment may be that we have forgotten that we have been commissioned to change the world.

This is part of our great mission. But we seem to

have lost sight of it in so many ways, and we seem obsessed with maintenance and survival. Mission or maintenance? This is the question that our times are laying at the feet of the Catholic Church. I hope with all my heart that we choose to mobilize around our great mission once again.

Nothing drives engagement like a worthy mission, and we certainly have that.

Imagine what we could achieve if we mobilized. There are seventy-seven million Catholics in the United States today. Catholics could determine every presidential election in this country. We could direct the outcome of almost every election at any level in this country. Catholics could determine the success or failure of almost any product or company. We could direct legislation, influence the types of movies that are made, control the nature of television programming that is produced, and put an end to poverty in America. If we could get our act together . . .

But instead, the last remaining socially acceptable prejudice in America is to be anti-Catholic. In our hypersensitive, politically correct culture, which preaches tolerance as the ultimate twenty-first-century virtue, everything is tolerated from the perverse to the insane, but not Catholicism. Tolerance is extended to all except Christians and their beliefs. These are seemingly intolerable.

We need to wake up. We have been fooled into believing that we are some quirky little fringe group. We can and should be a force to be reckoned with. Why do you think we are attacked so much? Those who oppose the Catholic worldview are afraid of how much influence we would have if we did ever actually get our act together.

And while it is important that we consider our worldly influence, and it is critical that we do get our act together in this respect, it is also crucial that we don't make these things an end in and of themselves. The worldly influence we are called to exert can so easily distract us from our primary mission of helping people discover God and walk with him.

So, changing the temporal world is not the primary way we are called to exert our influence. I use worldly examples to demonstrate what is possible. But we need to focus first and foremost on becoming men and women of virtue and character, and leading others to do the same. Every good thing we hope for the world will flow from the reemergence of character and virtue in our lives and in society.

The Best Way to Live

How is the best way to live? Every great civilization has concerned itself with this question. It is the primary question that the great philosophers of every age have grappled with. It is the question every culture, country, generation, and individual (consciously or unconsciously) wrestles with. It is one of the questions that are at the core of any spiritual quest. But perhaps most important, it is a question you and I grapple with in a deeply personal way at every juncture of our lives.

The rigor with which a person or culture approaches this question is very telling. It is of disturbing importance to note that the present culture has virtually no interest in pursuing it. Today we are more interested in how we want to live than we are in discovering the best way to live, just as we are much more interested in defending self-expression than we are in developing selves that are worth expressing. Personal preference has triumphed over the pursuit of excellence. We want what we want, and we feel entitled to it.

But the question remains: How is the best way to live? Though perhaps we need to consider another question in order to come to fully answer this one: Are some ways of living better than others? Our hyper-relativistic culture says no. We are told that the best way to live is different for every person, but that is only partially true.

Certainly we cannot consider this question in a vacuum. It must be pondered in a real place and time, for a specific person, with roles and responsibilities, needs, hopes, and desires. With this in mind we tend to leap straight to the conclusion that the best way to live is different for everyone. But is it? The answer, I think, is yes and no. A more strategic approach to this ageless question should consider what is common to everyone before we leap to what is unique to each individual.

On some level the best way to live is the same for all of us. Let us consider these three principles that are common to all men and women of goodwill.

The First Principle. The first principle is simply this: You are here to become the-best-version-of-yourself. Surely we can all agree that you are not here to become a-second-rate- version-of-yourself, that it is better to explore your potential than to squander it. Nor are you here to be another version of your parents, teachers, friends, or siblings. At some very basic foundational level God has created you and put you here on earth to be yourself. But being yourself is much more difficult than most would suppose, because it requires the real work of self-discovery. It also requires that you die unto your lesser self, so that in Christ your better self can emerge. Nonetheless, in this you share a common bond with all men, women, and children, for we are all here to become the-best-version-of-ourselves. The best way to live, therefore, is in ways that help you become the-best-version- of-yourself.

This first principle serves not only as a basis upon which to be- gin to answer the question about the best way to live but also as a very practical guide to the choices that make up everyday life. In fact, I would go so far as to say that everything in life makes sense in relation to this single principle. Embrace everyone and everything that helps you become a-better-version-of-yourself and you will live a life uncommon.

Everything makes sense in relation to the first principle. Life is about saying yes to the things that help you become the-best- version-of-yourself and no to the things that don't. It is not more complicated than that. Of course, we manage to complicate life substantially more. On a different plane of thinking the concept becomes a thing of beauty, for we finally realize that anyone or anything that does not help us to become a-better-version-of-our-selves is just too small for us. What liberation and joy we experience when we make this truth our own for the very first time.

This concept of celebrating the-best-version-of-ourselves at each moment and in each situation throughout the day brings the philosophical question "How is the best way to live?" to a very real and practical level. As our awareness grows we become mindful that we are constantly making choices and that every choice causes us to become a-better-version-of-ourselves or a-lesser-version-of-ourselves.

It is a natural extension that the best way to live also includes living your life in ways that help others to become the-best-version-of-themselves. Whenever we cause others to become a-lesser-version-of-themselves we are not at our best, and we are not living our best possible life. To prevent someone else from becoming the-best-version-of-themselves—now, that is a sin.

If we accept the first principle, then the meaning-of-life conversation becomes a fairly short one. You are here to become the-best-version-of-yourself. It is by knowing, loving, and serving God and neighbor that we become all he created us to be. We all have this in common, and so the best way to live on a macro level is the same for everyone. We are here to become the-best-version-of-ourselves. And so, on one level the answer to the question "How is the best way to live?" is the same for us all.

The Second Principle. As we continue to explore the best way to live, we will discover that it is not as different from person to person as one might first think. For thousands of years great minds including Plato, Aristotle, Augustine, Aquinas, Duns Scotus, Descartes, Immanuel Kant, Marcus Aurelius, Epictetus, and others have each in their own way held that "virtue" is the best way to live.

Every culture, country, and organization has an organizing principle. For Hitler's Germany it was tyranny. For China it is Communism. For Castro's Cuba it is dictatorship. For the United States it is law, which supports democracy and capitalism. For many companies it is reward. For some organizations it is excellence or contribution. For others it is fear. But what is the ultimate organizing principle—for your life, your family, an organization, a country, or indeed, the whole world? Virtue. Not necessarily in a religious sense, but simply in the classical Greek sense of the word.

Consider this. Two patient people will always have a better relationship than two impatient people. Two generous people will always have a better relationship than two selfish people. Two courageous people will always have a better relationship than two cowardly people. Two humble people will always have a better relationship than two prideful people. And every aspect of society—a family, a community, an organization, or even foreign relations between two nations—is an extension and multiplication of this single relationship.

Think of it this way. Who would you prefer as your employees or colleagues—men and women of virtue or those riddled with vice and selfishness? Would you prefer your neighbors be patient or impatient? Would you rather your extended family were generous or self-serving? Would you prefer honest or dishonest customers? Would you rather have a courageous or a cowardly manager?

The whole world prefers virtue.

Our present culture likes to say that virtue is a personal matter. Indeed, in some ways it is, but the impact of the virtue (or lack of virtue) of any one person cannot be confined to that person. Our words and actions, though personal, have real consequences on the lives of other people. These consequences are never confined to the individual. If one man shoots another man, the shooter's actions impact not only the man who is shot, but also that man's wife and children, his mother and father, brothers and sisters, friends and neighbors. Every good thing he may have done for the rest of his life will go undone. He may have been the person who was going to cure cancer. In the same way, if you help someone to find a job, your loving actions help that person, but also his (or her) family and the local community in so many ways it is impossible to measure. There are no purely personal acts. Everything we say, do, and think affects other people.

Virtue is the ultimate organizing principle, whether it is in a person's life, a marriage, or the life of a nation. And so, in virtue, we have another example of how the best way to live is the same for us all.

The Third Principle. The third principle is simply self-control. The best way to live is with self-control, which may very well be man's highest need. Without it we are rendered incapable of any sustainable success in life, business, relationships, or spirituality. For without self-control we are incapable of delaying gratification. Individualism, hedonism, relativism, and minimalism, the dominant practical philosophies of our age, all lead to the decay of humanity's self-control and the demise of our ability to delay gratification.

There is no success without the ability to delay gratification. What happens to someone's personal finances if they cannot delay gratification? What type of relationships is a person likely to have if he or she is unwilling to delay gratification? What quality of work can you expect from a person who is unable to delay gratification? What will happen to the health and well-being of a person who refuses in every instance to delay gratification? And you simply cannot grow spiritually if you refuse to delay gratification.

To be clear, I am not saying that we should always delay gratification. God wants us to experience intense pleasure. I am simply saying that in order to live your best life the ability to delay gratification is a required skill. And although there is more to self-control than delayed gratification, the two are inseparably linked. A person who is unable to delay gratification is incapable of self-control. If you wish to increase your self-control and create a stronger mind and more resolute will, practice delaying gratification many times a day.

It is better to live with self-control than it is to live without it. Here we have another example of how the best way to live is the same for us all.

So, to recap: 1) You are here to become the-best-version-of- yourself; 2) virtue is the ultimate organizing principle; and 3) self-control is central to the best way to live. In these three principles we find the common elements that bind us all together in our quest to answer the question "How is the best way to live?" It is better to live in a way that helps you become the-best-version-of- yourself than to live in a way that diminishes you and makes you less than who you are. It is better to live a life of virtue than a life of vice. And it is better to live with self-control than without it.

It is also important to note that most people's knowledge of and dedication to these three principles is minimal. At the same time most people's dedication to the philosophies of individualism, hedonism, relativism, and minimalism dwarfs their commitment to these three principles. Therein lies the challenge for anyone who wants to change the world.

It is true, however, that the answer to the question is in some ways different from person to person, and it changes for an individual at different times of his or her life.

The best way for a single person to live may legitimately be very different from the best way for a married person to live. One of my passions is helping young people discover their mission in life. When I have the chance to speak to high school and college students, one of my regular themes surrounds embracing "singleness."

We never have a better opportunity to serve than when we are single. Most people go on to marry, and marriage brings with it a series of commitments and responsibilities that limit our ability to serve people, causes, and organizations beyond our immediate duties. But in our singleness, we can serve generously, almost without reserve, and in ways that would not be possible for a married person.

On a personal level, when I was single the best way for me to live was to be actively involved in a variety of community and charitable organizations. Now that I am married and raising my family, I would be irresponsible as a husband and father to be involved in all these volunteer activities to the same extent. It would not be the best way to live, because it would be giving priority to something that is secondary. My primary responsibilities now are as a husband and a father.

In the same way, the best way to live can change as we move through the various seasons of life. What is the best way to live at twenty years old may differ at forty, fifty, or sixty. This is true even though our primary roles and responsibilities may not change in these different stages of life.

And so, by delving into the question of the best way to live, we quickly discover that it is not a question that we ask once, answer once, and are finished with. It is a dynamic question that requires a little bit of our attention every day for the rest of our lives.

Jesus was essentially asked this question once. One day while he was teaching in the temple he was approached by some of the religious leaders of his time. In an attempt to trick him, they asked him which was the greatest of the commandments. Jesus replied, "Love the Lord your God with all your heart, with all your soul, and with all your mind . . . and love your neighbor as yourself." (Matthew 22:37–39) And in doing so he also answered the question "How is the best way to live?"

The entire Gospels are an expanded answer to this question. In a sense every person who approaches Jesus is looking for the best way to live, just as you and I are constantly seeking the best way to live whether we are conscious of it or not.

The life of the Church and her teachings are an extension of the Gospel in that they too try to lead us toward the best way to live. As the ages have unfolded, new situations and questions have arisen, and men and women of goodwill have come to the Church and asked, "How is the best way to live in respect to this particular circumstance?" These answers all come together into an incredible body of knowledge and wisdom and are available to all people of all times.

Often people think that the Church says, you have to do this or you cannot do that. In fact, the Church does no such thing. The Church simply stands in every place and time pointing out the path toward the best way to live. Each of us gets to decide if we are going to walk that path or not.

And this is where we get to the heart of the matter. It is here that a new question arises: Do you believe that Jesus offers us the best way to live? If you don't believe that the life, teachings, and person of Jesus lead to the best way to live, who or what does? If you do believe that Jesus leads us in the best way to live, then isn't it a natural consequence that you want to share that best way with others? And that is Evangelization—helping other people to discover the love of God and the wisdom of his ways; helping people to live their best possible life and become the-best-version- of-themselves, helping people to discover the best way to live.

We want these things for anyone we love.

Jesus invites us to a life of love. How much do we really love? Sure, we love the people close to us. But most of the time, the giving and receiving go on in equal measure in these relationships. How often do we love and expect nothing in return? How often do we do something out of love that requires us to make sacrifices?

Evangelization is the ultimate form of love of neighbor. Is there any greater way to love your neighbor than by helping him or her discover the best way to live?

Are some ways of living better than others? Our relativistic culture says all ways of living are equal, but this is nonsense. We are told in this age of secularism that we should respect everybody's right to live however they wish, but how is that working out for us? Isn't this already a failed experiment? Relativism leads to a world where nobody is the-best-version-of-themselves. Were Mother Teresa's approach to life and Hitler's approach to life equal? I think not. One was better than the other. Relativism is the enemy of Evangelization, because if all ways of living are equal, then there is no need to lead others to a better life. Even the most casual observer comes to the conclusion upon reflection that some ways of living are better than others, and if that is the case, then there must be a best way of living. And if some ways of living are better than others, shouldn't we do what we can to help as many people as possible discover the best way to live?

I find it fascinating that we almost never talk about Heaven and hell anymore. What do you think happens when we die? Do you believe in Heaven? I do. My reasons are not as theological as some might expect. You see, I believe that this life is just a dim reflection of some infinitely greater reality. In my life I have experienced moments of incredible ecstasy—times of deep prayer and meditation, finding the person to spend my life with, the birth of my children, and to a lesser extent moments in travel, standing before truly beautiful art, a perfect golf shot—but these moments are fleeting and impossible to hold on to. Nonetheless, I believe they provide a glimpse into what God has in store for us, a preview of sorts. I have also experienced the love of God and the love of others, and if I reflect on what it would be like to be constantly in those moments of incredible love it is not difficult for me to imagine what Heaven might be like. And yet, I know that whatever I can imagine is only a dim reflection of what actually is. My faith counsels me that no one is disappointed when they experience Heaven.

For the same reasons, I believe in hell. I have tasted this experience too. There have been moments of great darkness in my life, when evil felt all too close. More to the point, I have felt far from God at times. I have also witnessed other people who were possessed by a living hell on earth. And as horrific as these dark moments can be—in our own lives or as we witness them in the lives of others—I also believe that these are just a dim reflection of an infinitely darker reality.

And while we are at it, we might as well take a moment to discuss the concept of purgatory. I am a practical man. If I eat too many doughnuts or french fries, I gain weight. In order to return to optimal health, I then have to exercise vigorously and abide by a rather strict diet. It would seem to me that the same is true spiritually. If I indulge in a vice on a regular basis my spiritual health is diminished. This vice affects my spiritual and physical health, my relationships, my intellectual clarity, and many other aspects of life, most of which I am probably not even aware of. Perhaps one day I decide to stop partaking in that vice. I may stop today, but the effects of my previous bad behavior will live in me for some time to come. It is only by the consistent and persistent practice of virtue that I may over time do away with the residual bad effects of my previous life of vice.

Now consider, what is Heaven? We may all have different ideas, but most can agree that it is a perfect state or experience. If you place something that is imperfect in something that is perfect, the whole becomes imperfect. For example, if you have a glass of pure olive oil and you add a drop of motor oil, you no longer have a glass of olive oil. I'm not sure what you have, but it is not olive oil. The glass of pure olive oil is Heaven; the drop of motor oil is something less than perfect—you and I. We can probably agree that most people are not the-best-version-of-themselves when they die, and so purgatory (an experience of purification) is just a natural and necessary consequence. Otherwise, adding something imperfect to something that is perfect would diminish it all.

When we do get to Heaven, I suspect there will be many surprises. Among these surprises, I think most people will be astounded to learn how much they are loved and how lovable they are. But we digress. If Heaven does exist, don't you want as many people as possible to experience it?

Win, Build, Send

Imagine you discovered the best way to live, and you wanted to change the world by helping as many people as possible to discover and live that best way. How would you go about it? Anyone who has any experience in marketing products or ideas will tell you that you need a system, and the best systems are simple. As it turns out, God has had a system in place from the very beginning. God wants to win you with his love and wisdom; God wants to build you up spiritually so that you have the knowledge and habits to live in his love and walk in his ways; and God wants to send you out into the world to share his love with others. Win. Build. Send.

God's plan for changing the world is to get as many people as possible to live the Gospel, which as we have just discovered turns out to be the best way to live. But first and foremost, he desires a dynamic and intimate friendship with us. Think about that. We are talking about the Creator of the universe here. If the President of the United States, the future King of England, or your favorite celebrity wanted to have a dynamic friendship with you, you would be flattered and enthusiastic. God wants to have an intimate friendship with you.

WIN

As I began to explain in the previous section, when I was about fifteen years old, I was tremendously fortunate that a handful of people helped me discover the genius of Catholicism. I really don't know where I would be today, or what I would be doing, if they had not taken the time to help me develop spiritually. My story is not as dramatic as others, it is simply a story of dissatisfaction with the life and ideas that the culture was serving up. It was a classic case of "there must be more to life."

One of the most intriguing things about Catholicism is that once you get a taste of the real thing it is absolutely fascinating and incredibly beautiful. Looking back, I think I was won for Christ and his Church by a single idea: We are all called to live holy lives. Of course, I was not won the first time I heard the idea. On paper it seems like an intimidating concept, but this became an organizing thought. Everything seemed to fall into place around this idea. There were certain ways to think, speak, and behave that caused me to grow in goodness, virtue, and holiness. There were other ways to think, speak, and behave that did not. This just seemed like common sense to me when I was encouraged to think about it. I had simply never been encouraged to think about it in such a compelling way. No great leap of faith was required. On a very natural level it seemed logical and practical.

From a purely selfish point of view, I noticed that when I was walking with God, and living the life he invites us all to live through the Gospels, I was happier. Happiness and holiness are intimately connected. In fact, I would go so far as to say that you cannot have one without the other. The connection between right-action and human happiness was unmistakable to me even as a teenager. I also noticed that the more I tried to live the life God was inviting me to, the more I became genuinely myself. And so, you can see where the phrase "the-best-version-of-yourself" came from. It is simply an attempt to put into the language of our age the dream that God has for all his children: that we grow to become all he created us to be.

It is also important to point out that I was not won once and for all. None of us are. We are human beings and as such we tend to vacillate, sometimes even in our most noble convictions. We are constantly engaging and disengaging. We go to and fro, even in important matters. Our love and allegiance, unlike God's, are not constant. At times I am filled with great doubts about aspects of our faith, while at other times I am filled with an almost absolute faith. There are times when I am on the verge of depression thinking about how human weakness in the Church has devastated the faith of so many people. At other times I am supremely confident that God is guiding all things in the life of the Church.

Just when I think I cannot love my wife any more than I already do, she will win me in new and unexpected ways, and it can be the simplest things that raise my love to a new level. I saw her reading to our daughter the other day. Isabel is just nine months old, but she loves having books read to her. She was so animated as Meggie read to her, and I thought to myself, what an incredible mother she is. In the same way, God wins me anew time and time again. There are things that happen every year that cause me to fall in love with his way more than ever before. What I am trying to say is that God does not win us just once. He wins us over and over again, in new and deeper ways. It is import-ant that we understand this; otherwise we can fall into the trap of thinking that the Win, Build, Send model is a one-time progression. This would leave us susceptible to saying that, because we have not yet been won or built completely we are not ready to be sent. Some of the smartest people I know get completely trapped in the win stage, and go around and around in circles for years. Others resist the send stage, saying that they have not been built sufficiently yet. The build and send stages will win you in new ways.

The biggest challenge I have faced in writing this book has been in trying to work out who the reader would be. Who are you? Man? Woman? Young? Old? Single? Married? Priest? Are you at the all-important moment in your life when you are searching for some clarity in the area of your faith? Are you hungry to grow spiritually? Are you already a highly engaged Catholic? Or perhaps you are a priest looking for solutions to the many complex challenges you face every day in the life of your parish. I don't know who you are, but I am not sure that matters. As long as you are willing to explore this question: Has Christ won you?

For most people the answer is in degrees. Most of us have been won to some extent. The question then becomes whether we are willing to let Jesus win us in new ways. I won't say I am completely won, although I hope eventually he wins me completely. If we allow him to win us over to his life and love a little more this year than last year, that is progress, spiritual progress—and that is a beautiful thing. Progress is never to be scoffed at, however slight it might be.

There are three ways people are won: through truth, beauty, and goodness. For some people it is the truth that shines forth from an intellectual search that wins their hearts for God. They read Thomas Aquinas and the beauty of truth and logic wins them over. For others, it is the beauty of the Sistine Chapel or Chartres Cathedral that wins their hearts for God. And for others still, it is the goodness of Christian service that wins them, when they witness Mother Teresa caring for an AIDS patient or they experience the goodness of Christian friendship, a friendship that has the other person's best interest at its core. Most of us are won by a combination of all three.

What's important to note is that if you examine the history of our faith and study the stories of millions of people who have come to a greater appreciation of Catholicism, while every person's story is unique, they have all come to Jesus through one of these three paths—truth, beauty, and goodness.

Among the highly engaged Catholics who were interviewed as part of this research, 89 percent described a conversion experience—an event in their life that won them to a more engaged relationship with God. Some of them used this language and described it as a conversion, but many of them described it with other language. Some simply said things such as, "That was when I really got it for the first time!" Some "got it" by going on a retreat, on a pilgrimage, or to a conference, others got it by reading a book or listening to a speech, and still others got it when they experienced a life-altering event or the death of a loved one.

We all need at least one really good conversion in our lives, but conversion is an ongoing process in the life of a Christian.

This I know for sure: We need to work out what exactly is the best way (or ways) to win modern Catholics for Jesus and his Church. It is clear when you talk to highly engaged Catholics that they get it. The way they think, speak, and live is markedly different from the rest of Catholics. When you speak to disengaged Catholics, it becomes clear quickly that they don't get it, and more important, I think, it is alarmingly clear that they never did get it.

For years now we have been doing research in preparation to build major programs for each of these Catholic Moments: Baptism, First Reconciliation, First Communion, Confirmation, Marriage Preparation, and RCIA. One thing that amazed me as we threw ourselves into this work was that there is no moment in the catechetical development of a Catholic who was baptized as a child when we ask him or her to make a choice for Christ and his Church. At every step along the way we assume that people are committed to Christ and his Church— but in too many cases that is a false assumption, and it is hurting us enormously. Without a commitment of some kind, it is so much easier to walk away— and people are walking away at an alarming rate. But they are not waking up one day and saying, "I am not going to church anymore." For most people it is not a conscious decision. Most people just drift away from the Church. They may have been going to church every week until one Sunday their child had a soccer tournament and they missed Mass. Before you know it, they are going three times a month or every second week. It continues in this way until they get completely out of the habit. But they come at Christmas, because it just feels like the right thing to do. That's how we're losing them. It's not because they delved into

Catholicism and discovered it has nothing to offer; it's not a well-informed and deliberate decision. They just drift away. This wouldn't be so rampant if our communities were stronger, because then we would notice they were drifting away, and we would throw them a lifeline. The point is, they are gone, tens of millions of them. But perhaps the more disturbing point is that when we had the chance, we never really won them. We never helped them to form an effective relationship with Jesus and his Church. They never really got it. If they did, they would never have left.

What programs in your parish are designed to win people for God and his Church? Sure, everything we do is capable of having that effect. But what do you do as a parish that is specifically and intentionally designed to win people? We need to spend a lot of time and energy working out how we are going to win people if we are going to breathe new life into the Catholic Church today.

Once again, it all starts at the level of personal transformation. God wins us one at a time. Have you been won? Are you open to being won? Do you need to be won again? God wants to win you in new ways today. I hope God is using this book to win you in new ways. And I hope we will get serious about creating opportunities for God to win men, women, and children in our parishes.

BUILD

It was through the friendship of one man in particular that I experienced the build stage. Highly engaged Catholics have built a spiritual life. Many of them have done it over the course of decades by trial and error and incredible persistence. They did it this way because nobody showed them the way. I consider myself incredibly blessed to have been coached by someone who had already done the hard work.

It all started, as I have written before, when

he encouraged me to stop by church for ten minutes each day on the way to school. It wasn't convenient, but this was a game changer for me. You can pray anywhere, but stop by your church for ten minutes each day for a week, and then tell me if it isn't different. This is where it all started for me. I know it sounds so basic—insignificant, almost. But game changers are usually simple.

After several weeks, during which I spent ten minutes each day at church just talking to God, my spiritual coach suggested I start reading the Gospels for fifteen minutes a day also. It was here that I really met Jesus in a comprehensive way for the first time. The Gospels had been part of my life for as long as I could remember. All through Catholic school they were read or referenced, and every Sunday I would hear the Gospel read, but it never resonated with me. But now, finally, the Gospels penetrated my heart and Jesus came to life.

Little by little, brick by brick, my friend was

helping me to build a spiritual life. He didn't thrust it all upon me at once. One at a time he introduced the key components of a vibrant spirituality. After several weeks of ingraining the habit of reading the Gospels, he suggested that I attend weekday Mass once a week. It was at daily Mass that I fell in love with the Mass . . . and I think it was through the daily Mass that I was won in a new way for the Church. I had been to Mass every Sunday of my life, but it was here in the daily Mass that it first really started to make sense. I have never been able to pinpoint exactly why that is, but there was something about the intimacy of that experience that allowed me to absorb it in a new way.

This spiritual friend was personally directing me in a process of continuous improvement.

Next, he suggested we spend a Saturday afternoon at a nursing home, visiting with those residents who rarely get visitors. Here I was introduced to the Christian tradition of works of mercy, which naturally draw us out of ourselves. One of the biggest obstacles to spiritual development is getting caught up in ourselves. Works of mercy effortlessly liberate us from this obstacle.

A few weeks later, he suggested that I go to Confession. I remember leaving that experience feeling elated, light as a feather, as if a great weight had been lifted from my back.

Throughout this entire process, week after week, I felt joy growing in my heart. I was happier, and in a very natural sense that was wonderful proof that I was on a new and important path.

Then one day, we were driving home from playing basketball, and he asked me if I would like to pray the rosary. I was embarrassed. My fourth and fifth grade teachers used to have us pray the rosary, but it had been years and I wasn't sure I remembered. He helped me through it, and by some grace I began praying the rosary each day. This simple, humble, and ancient prayer has been the source of incredible peace for me over the years. It never ceases to amaze me how this prayer slows me down and focuses me when I have the discipline to practice it.

From time to time, perhaps every three weeks or so, my friend would give me a spiritual book. By now I was devouring them. I was hungry to learn more. I felt like this great treasure had been before me my whole life, but I had essentially been ignoring it. I remember feeling angry that other people in my life had not helped me to discover it before now, and at the same time I felt grateful that I was experiencing it now.

But perhaps the most important aspect of my journey was one of the main points from part one. This one man helped me find answers to my questions. I had questions about prayer, I had questions about the Mass, I had questions about things I was reading in the Bible, questions about things I was reading in spiritual books, questions about things I would hear about Catholicism in the media. I had questions about life and he helped me discover answers to those questions.

I learned so much from him in this regard. He taught me that you don't have to have all the answers to help someone else grow in the faith; you just have to be willing to help him or her find the answers to the questions you cannot answer. He taught me that there are answers to the questions. In the process, I came to one of my most strongly held convictions about our faith: People deserve answers to their questions.

At every step in the process, I was being built up in knowledge and experience of God, and in every step I was being won in new and deeper ways.

You will notice that I mention process several times. It was a process. The man who was guiding me wasn't acting on a whim; he was intentionally sharing the faith with me and trying to lead me to a better life—the best life, in fact. He had spent decades developing a vibrant and practical spirituality for himself, and now he was freely sharing the wisdom of his experience. I was blessed to know him.

God wants to build in you a dynamic spirituality. He wants our parishes to help people of all ages build a spiritual life, so that through our regular spiritual routines he can build and refine us in his image.

It is not enough for us to hope that this happens. We need process and intentionality. These are two of the key ingredients of effective evangelization. It isn't just going to happen. We need a plan.

SEND

The mistake here would be to focus on my public life as a speaker and writer. This work is certainly evangelization, but very few of us are called to evangelize in that way. We are, however, all called to evangelize. And the truth is, it is much easier to speak and write for large audiences than it is to take an interest in helping a few people whom God has placed in our lives to grow spiritually.

My first attempts at sharing the faith with others were clumsy and awkward. I was a teenager. My friends were interested in what teens are interested in. My best friends listened respectfully. My not-so-good friends dismissed my efforts out of hand. Most of all, I was impatient.

Over the years, my approach to attracting people to Christ and his Church has become much more natural and patient. There are three keys to this approach: friendship, generosity, and answers.

Friendship is the most natural and effective way to share the faith with others. If we are friends and I say something that you disagree with, you are not likely to dismiss it without consideration. Out of the respect that is built through the course of a friendship, you will consider my point of view, even if you disagree with it. Inviting people to explore their questions of faith in a new way is asking them to rethink the way they live their lives—often in major ways. It is the respect that is born through friendship that allows people to let their guard down and consider a new way.

Christian friendship is not just about common interests; it is about helping each other become the-best-version-of-ourselves. A friendship that places the other person's best interests above our own selfish desires or agenda is quite rare in this world. Often when people first experience this kind of friendship, they don't believe it. Christian friendship seems too good to be true in the current cultural landscape. And so, it takes time to convince people that our friendship is genuine and rightly motivated. But it is this type of friendship that becomes the vehicle for the faith to spread.

The second key to Evangelization is generosity. Christianity, by its very nature, is generous. We are called to be generous with our time, talent, and treasure, but also with our love and compassion, going out of our way to generously serve those who cross our path. Generosity is disarming and attractive.

The third key, and in some ways the most important at this time in the life of the Church and culture, is helping people find answers to their questions. I cannot stress this point enough. We live in a time when more people have questions about Catholicism than ever before. Catholics have questions and non-Catholics have questions. One of the most effective ways to evangelize is to help people articulate their questions and help them to find answers to those questions. This form of evangelization becomes deeply personal, because it drives straight at the obstacles holding a person back from surrendering his or her life to God. Fulton Sheen wrote, "There are only one hundred people in the world who disagree with what the Church teaches. The rest disagree with what they think the Church teaches."

Ignorance is massive, and above most things I believe that people deserve answers to their questions. It is amazing how once we get a taste of the truth, we develop an insatiable appetite for it. Once we catch a glimpse of the beauty of truth, the shallowness and emptiness of our culture is revealed.

We are all being called to share our faith with others. Through the beauty of Christian friendship, the goodness of outrageous generosity, and answering people's deepest questions, we are able to invite people to discover God, his Church, and the best way to live.

***

Win. Build. Send. This is the process of Evangelization. Too often when we talk about Evangelization in the Catholic Church, we are asking people who have not been sufficiently won and built to go out into the world on a mission, and they are simply not ready. Most Catholics don't evangelize because they don't actually believe that Catholicism is a superior way of life. So why would they want to share it? They have not been won. Until we are won, we don't have the passion, that fire in our belly, to attract anyone else—and Christianity only genuinely grows through attraction.

Of late, we have been talking about the New Evangelization. It is a theme that was first proposed by John Paul II and one that has been further emphasized by Benedict XVI. But here in the United States one has to question if there was an old evangelization. The Church in America has for the most part only ever grown by birth, marriage, and immigration. Though it is waning now, the luxury of a vibrant birth rate and large numbers of Catholic immigrants allowed the Church to appear to be strong and growing. In truth, the Church in the United States has always grown, but not because we were committed to sharing the genius of Catholicism with others—and not because we are particularly good at it. The percentage of true converts who make up the growth of the Catholic Church in America is minuscule, especially if you take out those who converted in order to marry a Catholic.

The reason I share this is because if we are ever going to get really good at Evangelization, it is critical to recognize that we have never been particularly good at it.

The Win, Build, Send model works. And perhaps what it points out best is that we have been trying to accomplish this great mission of our Church—Evangelization—without a model. We need a model that is scalable and sustainable. There are no shortcuts. There is no point trying to send people if they have not been sufficiently won and built. This always ends in disaster. So, when we talk about new efforts in the area of Evangelization, it is impossible to have any real conversation without also considering what are we going to do to increase our success at winning and building people.

People don't fail because they want to fail. They fail because they don't know how to succeed. In terms of Evangelization, we have never really trained people how to do it. We need a process for training Catholics to become really good at sharing the genius of Catholicism with others.

Everyone evangelizes about something, but most of us evangelize about the wrong things. Have you seen how passionate some people are when they talk about their iPhone? They tell you why they love it so much, point out the favorite apps and features, and by the time they are finished you probably want one yourself. That is evangelization. Other people evangelize about their car, their company, or their favorite vacation destination. It's amazing how animated we can become about things that are trivial. It is in our nature to evangelize. Sadly, many people have nothing better than their iPhone or favorite vacation place to evangelize about.

We are all evangelists. What are you evangelizing about?

Feeling Good About Being Catholic

Throughout the Win and Build stages, one of the things that happens to people is that they start to feel good about being Catholic. We don't talk anywhere near enough about this. In the context of a theological discussion or Church governance this might seem a little soft, but it is absolutely essential to the life and growth of the Church. Highly engaged Catholics feel good about being Catholic. They are inspired Catholics.

There are always reasons to feel down about our Catholic identity. Our own time is no different, and one of the costs of the sexual abuse scandal is that it has robbed many ordinary people of their ability to feel good about being Catholic. Tragically, while the media has attacked us relentlessly because of the sexual abuse scandals, we have not responded. We have not made our story known. We have allowed ourselves to be engulfed by negativity and failed to demonstrate our incredibly positive contributions.

In every place and time there is no shortage of reasons to feel really good about being Catholic. These include our social and spiritual contributions, the life we bring to communities, and the support we provide physically, emotionally, intellectually, and spiritually to literally hundreds of millions of people around the world every day. Our education and health care systems are just two examples. The list is endless but, sadly, little known. Ask Catholics to tell you three really great things about their Church and you quickly discover how little most people know about the role the Church plays in so many people's lives.

It is not that the good justifies the bad; rather, it is that the good is the result of authentically living the Catholic faith, while the bad reflects the fallibility of human beings. The bad usually says more about human nature than it does about the Catholic faith.

It is impossible to share the goodness and beauty of Christ and his Church with others if you don't feel good about being Catholic. So, we'd better start spending some time thinking about this question: What will it take to get ordinary Catholics to feel good about being Catholic again?

The thing I have learned in all the years I have been speaking and writing is that people don't do anything until they are inspired. You can have all the right words on the page, but if people are not inspired, they won't respond to those words. Over the past twenty years, there have been enormous efforts to make sure that we are teaching the truth of the Catholic faith in our faith formation programs, but in too many cases these programs are dry and uninspiring—so people don't respond. What were the disciples doing between the death of Jesus and Pentecost? Not much. What did they do after Pentecost? They changed the world. Seriously, these twelve guys literally changed the world. What happened? They got inspired. I realize that is not the theological jargon for what happened, but that's what happened. Catholics today need to be inspired. We need a massive outpouring (and inpouring) of the Holy Spirit.

People don't do anything until they are inspired, and once people are inspired there is almost nothing they can't do. Inspiring people is critical and something we have overlooked for too long.

Not surprisingly, the research discovered that Dynamic Catholics feel good about being Catholic. And they feel this way about Catholicism regardless of what is happening in their parish, regardless of the latest Church scandal, and regardless of how Catholicism has been distorted or abused throughout history. Catholicism is bigger than all this for them.

Again, let me stress, this is no small thing and not to be discounted.

One of the things I noticed very early on about the Dynamic Catholic Parish Book Program was that the excitement of passing out all those books to parishioners at Christmas and Easter just makes people feel good about being Catholic. I have noticed the same thing about different Catholic television ad campaigns. Often these advertisements are aimed at bringing people back to church, but I think we overlook or discount the tremendous value they have in inspiring those who do come to church every Sunday to feel good about being Catholic. From time to time, you need to encourage those who are faithful, and it turns out that is one of the most effective ways to win back the disengaged.

How many Catholics are really proud to be Catholic? The truth is, morale is very low among Catholics today, and if we cannot change that, our ability to evangelize is going to be limited. You don't try to share something with others unless you feel really good about it yourself. And this might be the heart of the problem. The truth we are unwilling to face may just be that most Catholics don't feel good about being Catholic.

Beyond this overall feeling about being Catholic, the research surrounding the fourth sign of a Dynamic Catholic unveiled some interesting findings. First, even among highly engaged Catholics, Evangelization is the weakest link in the chain. When asked to rate themselves between 1 and 10 for each of the four signs, the 7% rated themselves at 6.8 or higher for Prayer, Study, and Generosity, but at just 4.9 for Evangelization.

When asked if they considered themselves evangelists, the overwhelming number of respondents said no. When asked to name an evangelist, more than 85 percent of highly engaged Catholics cited a non-Catholic evangelical Christian preacher. It is of significant interest to note that throughout the course of the interviews the most common person mentioned in any context was John Paul II. But when interviewees were asked who is an evangelist, John Paul II was not mentioned. This was particularly surprising to me, considering the fact that he preached the Gospel to more people than any other person in history.

So, even though Evangelization is a core behavior among highly engaged Catholics, they tend to do it in a more passive way than one might expect. One question they were asked was, "What is the best Catholic book you have ever read?" After they responded they were then asked what they had done with the book after they had finished reading it. Invariably, they would say something like, "Oh, I gave that book to my friend Susie at work." In a very natural and nonthreatening way they were trying to share the faith with other people in their circle of influence by passing along books.

When Dynamic Catholics were asked what they did to try to share the faith with others, their top six answers were:

Give people great Catholic books.

Invite people to Catholic events.

Bring a godly perspective to conversations.

Learn the Catholic teachings on certain issues and be able to articulate them when the Church is attacked over those issues in social settings.

Help people discover answers to the questions that cause them to doubt the Catholic faith.

Demonstrate the love of God through faithful and generous friendship.

When asked about their first conscious attempts to share the faith with others, they all described the challenge of going beyond their comfort zone and seemed to be in consensus that the first efforts were anxious and awkward attempts at evangelization.

Astoundingly, when asked if anyone had ever

taught them how to evangelize, 99.4 percent of respondents said no.

But what was demonstrated over and over throughout the research is that the first and second signs (Prayer and Study) tend to give birth to the third and fourth signs (Generosity and Evangelization). The fourth sign cannot be increased in isolation. The first three signs make the fourth possible.

In summary, I think the research points out good and bad news in the area of Evangelization. The bad news is that as Catholics in America we are doing a very poor job of evangelizing the society we live in today. The good news is that we have never really tried. Most Catholics have never been taught how to evangelize in any systematic way, nor have they been convinced why they should do it.

The future of Evangelization depends upon our ability to win people for Christ and his Church, to build people in Christ and his Church, and to develop programs that teach people how to evangelize. Only then will we be able to send them out to change the world in any meaningful way.

Contagious Living

When it comes to Evangelization it seems that every Catholic's favorite quote is from Francis of Assisi: "Preach the Gospel at all times and when necessary, use words." There are two things to consider here. First, he did say to preach the Gospel at all times. Second, he didn't say never to use words. The quote is used too often as an excuse not to preach the Gospel, and especially not to actively evangelize.

Evangelization is to the Church what breathing is to a person. If we stop doing it for long enough, we will die. The Church has been on life support in this area for decades now. And the truth is, it is our mission to evangelize. We exist to evangelize. But we are neglecting it, and perhaps that is why our very existence in different places is being threatened. Isn't forgetting the reason for our existence the ultimate form of spiritual amnesia?

How do we start? We do so in the same way we are called to start with each of the four signs: with the smallest nonthreatening step. Incremental improvement can be applied to each of the four signs for incredible results.

The most fascinating thing about giving all the books away at Christmas and Easter was that inside the back of the book we placed an advertisement inviting people to visit DynamicCatholic.com if they liked the book and request six more copies at a very low cost. Every week we ship thousands of books in response to this simple ad. Some people might say, "That's great that you're selling a lot of books." Others might say, "That's fabulous that you're getting the message out to lots of people." But the real victory here is that we have given

Catholics a simple way to evangelize. People don't buy six copies for themselves—they are passing them around to family and friends.

You see, if we are honest with each other, I think we can agree that most Catholics are not too comfortable or competent talking about their faith with others. But what the little experiment above proves is that most Catholics are comfortable giving someone a book.

So, here is the action step: Try to do one thing each week to share the faith with someone who crosses your path. Perhaps you tell him you are going to pray for him and a situation he told you about. Perhaps you give her a book. Perhaps you try to present God's perspective in a conversation. Or maybe you invite someone to a Catholic event. Just do one thing each week. It could even be as simple as sharing a statistic or fact about Catholics with others: "Did you know that Catholic education saves the U.S. taxpayer eighteen billion dollars a year?" Or perhaps you sign up for Dynamic Catholic's daily e-mail and forward it to a different friend depending on the content.

If every member of your parish did one thing each week to share the faith with others, how different would your parish be a year from now? If every Catholic in America did just one small act of evangelization each week, how would the Church grow over the next decade?

Little by little we can have an enormous impact. Just don't let what you can't do interfere with what you can do. Are you going to have to step outside your comfort zone? Yes, but you can do that a little bit at a time also.

If you place a bucket under a dripping tap, what happens? Drop by drop the bucket fills up, and then it overflows. The Win and the Build aspects of the Catholic journey are the drops of water; the Send stage is the overflow. If the bucket is sound and the tap is dripping, eventually it has to overflow. It has no choice.

When Catholicism is lived enthusiastically and generously it is incredibly attractive. In this way our lives become contagious.

When it comes to Evangelization, it seems to me that again we are plagued by the "let's see what happens" approach. We are paralyzed by inaction. Perhaps it is because we don't know what to do or how to do it, but if that is genuinely the problem, then let's get serious about solving it. Perhaps it is because enough of us have not yet been sufficiently won and built.

We started with the question, "If you could change the world, what would you change?" Here's the thing. We can change the world, and you can play a role in it. In fact, no group or organization is in a better position to change the world than Catholics.

About the Author

MATTHEW KELLY is a bestselling author, speaker, thought leader, entrepreneur, consultant, spiritual leader, and innovator.

He has dedicated his life to helping people and organizations become the-best-version-of-themselves. Born in Sydney, Australia, he began speaking and writing in his late teens while he was attending business school. Since that time, 5 million people have attended his seminars and presentations in more than 50 countries.

Today, Kelly is an internationally acclaimed speaker, author, and business consultant. His books have been published in more than 30 languages, have appeared on the *New York Times*, *Wall Street Journal*, and *USA Today* bestseller lists, and have sold more than 50 million copies.

In his early-twenties he developed "the-best-version-of-yourself" concept and has been sharing it in every arena of life for more than twenty-five years. It is quoted by presidents and celebrities, athletes and their coaches, business leaders and innovators. Though perhaps it is never more powerfully quoted than when a mother or father asks a child, "Will that help you become the-best-version-of-yourself?"

Kelly's personal interests include golf, music, art, literature, investing, spirituality, and spending time with his wife, Meggie, and their children Walter, Isabel, Harry, Ralph, and Simon.

Visit **MatthewKelly.com** for his Blog
and so much more.

Subscribe to
Matthew's YouTube Channel!

www.youtube.com/matthewkellyauthor